WHY TELEPHONE COUNSELLING?

- Leveraging man's most important invention ever, to make more impact in business and ministry.

By
BISHOP O. INNOCENT.

Copyright reserved. No part of this book may be reproduced or copied in any way without the written permission of the publisher or author.

DEDICATION

This little book is dedicated to:

A mother in Israel,

DAMARIS FAULKNER

The Director of Missions,

International Fellowship of Christian Crisis Centers,

Minnesota, USA.

CHAPTER ONE

WHY COUNSELING AT ALL?

A large army of people are hurting world-wide. Many are worrying themselves sick without knowing whom to talk to or where to go in search of help. Many are withdrawing into themselves becoming social recluses and hermits. Others are developing medical complications such as high blood pressures, strokes and cardiac arrests while others, apparently not being able to take more or find needed help, choose either suicide or euthanasia.

Consider the following statistics:

Top of Form

 "One Million People Commit Suicide Each Year - World Suicide Prevention Day, September 10th, 2011

Published Saturday 10 September 2011

By Christian Nordqvist

"According to WHO, approximately one million people commit suicide each year worldwide, that is about one death every 40 seconds or 3,000 per day. For each individual who takes his/her own life, at least 20 attempt to do so. Suicide has a global mortality rate of 16 per 100,000 people.
 Dr. Berman said that suicide rates are considerably reduced when leaders make suicide prevention a top priority for their entire systems, as is the case in the US Air Force. When programs that concentrate on improving recognition and care of depression are implemented, the number of suicides and suicide attempts go down significantly.

Dr. Berman added:

Suicide is the tenth leading cause of death globally. In the USA there are two suicides for every homicide. Worldwide, the suicide rate has gone up by 60% over the last five decades - mainly in industrialized nations.

60% of all suicides occur in Asia. China India and Japan account for about 40% of all suicides, according to WHO.

16.5% of suicides in the USA are alcohol-related. An alcoholic has between 5 and 20 times the risk of committing suicide compared to the rest of the population. Individuals who misuse drugs are 10 to 20 times more likely to take their own lives. Approximately 33% of suicides among those younger than 35 years of age have a primary diagnosis of alcohol or other substance misuse. Among adolescent suicides, alcohol or drug misuse is factors in up to 70% of cases.

In Western countries, men commit suicide more often than women, but women attempt suicide more frequently. Experts say this is probably because men are more willing to end their lives through effective violent means. In the majority of countries throughout the world, drug overdoses make up approximately two-thirds of suicides among females and one-third among males."

Culled from:

https://www.medicalnewstoday.com/articles/234219.php

Another professional body confirms this statistics and more:

Suicide Statistics

Suicide is the tenth leading cause of death in the US, accounting for more than 1% of all deaths. It is the second leading cause of death among people ages 15-24. [4]

More years of life are lost to suicide than to any other single cause except heart disease and cancer [5]

44,000 Americans die by suicide each year. There are 13.8 deaths by suicide per 100,000 persons each year. [6]

There is one death by suicide for every 25 attempts [7]

40% of persons who complete suicide have made a previous attempt. [8]Nine of out ten people who attempt suicide and survive, do not go on to complete suicide at a later date. [9]

Previous suicide attempts serve as a risk factor for completed suicide. Suicide risk is 37% higher in the first year after deliberate self-harm than in the general population. Older white adults have triple the suicide risk than younger, non-white adults. [10]

Suicide rates are highest among adults between 45 and 64 at 19.6 percent. The second highest rate is 19.4 among those 85 years or older. Compared with middle-aged older adults, younger populations have consistently lower suicide rates. While males are four times more likely to do die by suicide, females are three times more likely to attempt suicide. [11]

Those with substance abuse disorders are six times more likely to complete suicide than those without. The rate of completed suicide among men with alcohol/drug abuse problems is 2-3 times higher than among those without a problem.

http://www.mentalhealthamerica.net/suicide

Suicide mentality may not be the only reason why people need counseling but it is surely a pointer to the fact that people are hurting generally. If according to the statistics above, as much as 44,000 persons as at 2011 commit suicide every year in USA with all the social amenities in this country, you can imagine the number that are quietly suffering worldwide.

People are suffering in many ways as we have seen above:

Many are suffering from substance abuse

Depression,

Broken marriages

Rejection.

Joblessness.

Ill health.

Financial challenges,

Mental problems.

Phobias.

Terminal diseases and a long list of other issues..

They all need healing. Forget the smiles and volcanic embraces that go on when folks meet 'friends' and acquaintances in public. Forget that couple you see going hand in hand in public with plastic smiles. Underneath it all, they may be hurting.

People are groaning inside while waiting for the earnest manifestation of counselors. These are people professionally trained or spiritually equipped to bring solution to the challenges faced by those who are hurting.

CHAPTER TWO

DEFINITION OF COUNSELING

By the way and in my own words, counseling is simply the communication of healing.

It starts with people being hurt and in need of a solution to the causes of their hurt or discomfort.

Understanding might be well served when we quote some more qualified authorities than this writer and what better place to start than with the academia?

The Stephen F. Austin State University defines counseling by first quoting the American Counseling Association and I have chosen to start with it because in so doing we will be killing two birds with one stone so to say. This is how the university puts it:

"Definition of Counseling

According to the American Counseling Association, counseling is defined as, "a professional relationship that empowers diverse individuals, families, and groups to accomplish mental health, wellness, education, and career goals." Counseling involves helping people make needed changes in ways of thinking, feeling, and behaving, and is a goal-based collaborative process, involving a non-judgmental, supportive counselor who works with a client in telling his or her story, setting viable goals, and developing strategies and plans necessary to accomplish these goals. For some people this process takes a small amount of time, in some cases as little as one or two sessions; for others, the process may last longer.

An extremely important part of counseling is confidentiality, which means that the information discussed in session will be accessible only by you and your counselor, with a few exceptions. Please see Client Confidentiality for more detail.

What Issues Does Counseling Address?

People come to counseling when their attempts to deal with their concerns are no longer effective. Counseling can be helpful areas such as:

Addiction and abuse of alcohol and other drugs

Adjustment issues, including adjustment to college life

Anger management

Anxiety

Communication

Depression

Eating disorders

Gender identity and sexual orientation

Grief

Relationship difficulties, including roommates, significant others, and professors

Relationship violence and physical abuse

Sexual assault

Stress management

Thoughts of suicide or preoccupation with death

Trauma"

Culled from: http://www.sfasu.edu/counselingservices/182.asp

Permit me to cite a second example. The "Business Directory" describes counseling as:

"Support process in which a counselor holds face to face talks with another person to help him or her solve a personal problem, or help improve that person's attitude, behavior, or character."

Read more: http://www.businessdictionary.com/definition/counseling.html

When we marry the three definitions above, we get a hold of the following facts:

People are hurting. The reason apart, people are hurting.

Those hurting are not restricted to any one location or country.

They need healing.

The world cannot afford to ignore those hurting.

Counseling remains one of the helpful tools to be used in answer.

Counseling is broad and different styles present different options.

Those trained and equipped for this communication of healing to the hurting, bringing lasting solutions to them are called Counselors.

WHO IS A COUNSELOR?

Counselors are people trained and equipped to identify cause or causes of anguish to people and remove them through communication of healing. This communication can be written, verbal, oral, non-verbal or psychological.

A person who goes to a counselor is wise because:

The bible says in the multiply of counsel, there is safety.

The counselor is trained and equipped to solve their problems.

They will have somebody to confide in.

They will be told where to go to for additional help.

They can win a friend in the counselor.

The counselor's intervention can stop other problems.

A counselor is also a coach who' helps us to bring out inner strength in the client.

When counseling is done by a Christian, or the counseling is Bible based, it becomes Christian Counseling. Some other schools of thought say that when the counseling institution is owned by a Christian or its staff dominated by Christian, then the counseling can be described as Christian Counseling.

THE SCOPE OF COUNSELING

Counseling in scope is wide depending on the nature, method or approach, who is being counseled [egg family counseling] and media employed but our focus here is just telephone counseling.

TELEPHONE COUNSELING

This as mentioned earlier, is communication of healing done via the telephone or mobile phone. This includes counseling done via the internet or what some people call e-counseling or online counseling.

Who needs Telephone Counseling?

Any man who needs in-person counseling can also benefit from telephone counseling. This includes all the sick and hurting people on earth. The only noticeable difference between the two types of counseling being that there is no eye contact in telephone conference but even that can be remedied with the use of such social media apps as Skype. Almost all the limitations of the in-person counselor are removed as can be seen from the points below.

CHAPTER THREE

WHY MORE PEOPLE NEED COUNSELING WORLD-WIDE

The world has need of counselors generally now more than ever before because problems of mankind seem to be growing by the day. Below are some of the reasons for this:

More People are being uprooted than before. Most unfortunately, more and more of the earth's eight billion humans are being **uprooted** from their environments. They are daily forced out of where they had been living for years through wrong global governmental policies. They now seek new homes as economic refugees whether legally or otherwise and most times their applications are turned down. The world naturally becomes a difficult place to understand because they are being uprooted for no cause of theirs. The one that gets the nod to move to greener pastures needs counseling to settle down. The one that fails the test needs counseling too, to understanding what is happening.

More people go to jail for what they cannot understand. People's right to freedom are being trampled upon and denied them world-wide. People are daily put in all kinds of prisons. A prison as you know is a place where we lose our right to decide for ourselves what to do at any given time.

Prisoners lack choice on things as basic as what to eat and what not to eat. A free person has the right to decide when to get up from the bed but a prisoner is regimented. So they go to bed when the jailers want and rise at either the sound of a bell or belt on their back.

Everyone in prison needs counseling on how to cope inside and outside when it comes time for him to go back into the society but the walls of prison keep them from getting both quality and choice counseling.

People are losing their paid jobs. A man who two years ago could feed his family three times a day but can no more put one meal on the table, is in a mess that denies his freedoms. Such a man is more or less in a mental prison. He also loses the right to choice since he lacks the purchasing power to buy what he wants. The right to go wherever he wants is also lost; since he cannot afford costs. Thanks to growing global inflation and economic recession the number of people in situations as mentioned above is daily surging forward in growth.

Many of these persons become traumatized, especially the highly skilled but jobless fellows. They need counseling but lack of funds keeps them at home. They too need counseling to enable them cope.

Wars continue to mushroom world-wide. The over-whelmed victims cannot understand what is happening. As we speak there is hardly a nation free from one war or the other. Houses and homes are being destroyed by the minute. Bombs are dropping on Iraq, Syria, Yemen, Congo, etc. People are being killed and/or maimed in one way or the other, leaving billions of people hurting and traumatized. They need counseling to cope but may are cut off from such help by flying bullets all around them. They cannot go to counselors and counselors cannot go to them for the same reasons. So telephone counseling comes to the rescue.

Intolerant regimes add to the problem world-wide. Internal strife continues to take its toll on mankind. As nations continue to implode and fragment, bitterness and all manners of heart diseases are tap-rooting. Billions of people are suffering. They want out but cannot leave their countries. People

 are hungry and in danger of starving and are actually losing their lives.

Indeed, Man's universal [basic] freedoms are being eroded. This is daily adding to the number of people who need help but cannot reach points and places where they can be helped by the in-person counselor. Here are some freedoms being denied world-wide and which create mental and physical refuge problems:

Freedom to choose.

Freedom to move about.

Freedom to expression.

Freedom to association.

Freedom to live without fear.

Freedom from hunger.

Freedom to live.

Freedom to worship.

Freedom to vote

Freedom to work and earn a living

INCREASING TERRORISM

This growing challenge needs special mention. It denies mankind the freedom of movement kills and maims. People with bitterness and violence as their gods are increasing by the day. There are growing cults of bitter amoral people who believe that the only thing that can make them happy is to kill, maim and disfranchise those who do not worship their gods with them. You must worship their poly gods or die.

They manufacture and export terrorism globally. They drop improvised explosive devises cowardly when people are not looking. They relish in suicide bombing and kidnapping spreading fear world-wide. In Nigeria, they are called **Boko Haram**. They are in Afghanistan as the **Taliban** and in Somalia as **Elshabab**, to mention only a few.

One of the fastest manufacturers of traumatized and disease prone people are the terrorists. They blaze through an area with great sound and fury, leaving behind sorrows, tears and blood. They are daily adding to the world-wide number of people hurting and needing counseling on how to cope.

Among the things that keep potential clients way from the in-person counselor, **XENOPHOBIA IS ON THE RISE.** This is the fear of foreigners. It makes foreigners to sit down in their own countries instead of travelling out in search of help such as counseling.

Xenophobia is a growing trend mostly in nations with corruption induced stunted growth. These countries are mostly those ones that cannot provide jobs and social welfare for the youths and in search of scapegoats, the politicians poison the minds of their youths against citizens of other nations. Fed with plenty lies by these bungling and fumbling politicians; the youths wax into mobs and attack every foreigner in sight as if killing them automatically creates jobs. Incidentally most of the menials jobs held by these foreigners are jobs indigenes do not want to touch preferring high–paying white collar jobs and high-sounding political jobs and empty titles.

Xenophobia leads not only to deaths and repatriations: foreigners are criminalized of leaving a large army of hurting people in its wake. Those who survive xenophobia attacks abroad not only become bitter but return to their own country with not just bitterness and frustration but vengeance and transferred aggression against innocent foreigners in the victim's own country. The world is truly hurting.

Another factor is religious bias. This refers to the non-violent but dissenting religious bigots. Their activities are making man to build mental walls around his family. In some African countries, children must not stray from one Christian denomination to another.

An elderly woman in Nigeria once told me that she was ex-communicated by the Catholic Church because her children, who are adults in their own night, converted to Pentecostalism. Some Islamic fanatics do not only throw stones at those who go outside the religion to seek help; not to talk of those who convert to other religious being spared.

The result is that people who are hurting but who could have gone to counselors in other religious or denominations are not able to do so because they fear the consequences of being seen by intolerant people with great bias. Thus, they remain in brick and mortar prisons called home.

Of cause such frustrating scenarios have led to suicides, transferred aggression, domestic violence, constant quarrels and divorces.

IGNORANCE :

Shocking as it is ignorance, continues to keep people in mental slavery to date. People do not know what to do when hurting. Those who know what, do not know how. People go to school these days to learn how to watch television and how to relate to computers. A cursory look at school curricula painfully reveals that less people are being admitted into courses on human relations.

What are we harvesting from the above? We have people with doctorate degrees in artificial intelligence for instance without the least understanding of how to show respect to a wife or women in general. They know next to nothing on how to relate with our information saturated, internet savvy kids. We produce professors of rocket science, who do not know how to say sorry when needed, even when they think they are right. The world as we know it today is full of people who are tall in academics but short in humanism. People are full of smiles but underneath they are hurting especially in ivory towers where science and technology have not wiped their tears.

Natural disasters are on the increase

As USA was heaving a sigh of relief after battling with high profile hurricanes, in Texas and Florida, Mexico became hard hit by a high scale quake that left about 250 persons dead. The Caribbean's were not left out by the devastating hurricanes. Neither did Australia and other nations in that region escape without a touch. Bush fires have erupted in places without known causes. Mudslides and endemic floods have hit Sierra Leone, Niger and Nigeria in recent times. People are rendered homeless and farm produce destroyed, creating hunger and disease.

Climate change continues to be the worst offenders here because these days, rain no longer falls- it pours! Fires no longer burn, they ravish. The atmosphere is saturated with disease causing smoke and chemical wastes. What goes around comes around as electronic wastes and inferior goods are dumped on back-ward nations and those nations in turn send their sick to the so-called first world.

Hate speeches are the order of the day.

There is too much fear in the world we are in today. Mutual fear and suspicion are creating a lot of casualties world-wide. In Rwanda, due to evil things one tribe was broadcasting against the other, Hutus and Tutsis rose up against me another in arms and almost half a million people were slaughtered in a week.

In Kenya, the tribes are at each other's throat not because they just discovered their differences. No lather, using the mass media and social media in particular, the people have made mountains out of moles, leading to bloodshed.

Hate speeches create high blood pressure and other associated diseases. People walk the streets not knowing when they will be attached for no fault of theirs but because they come from a particular tribe. People that have managed to escape across boundaries keep looking back wondering whether they had not made the greatest mistake of their lives.

Hate speeches, sometimes are state sponsored and lead to ethnic cleansing and growing frustration.

ECONOMIC REFUGEES

Many persons, particularly the near sighted, feel that the only way to survive or outwit poverty is to migrate in search of greener pasture. They forget that poverty is not the exclusive reserve of any region of the world. Most countries of the world are lands of diversity with both the extremely rich and ultra-poor.

As a result, thousands of people have died, trying to cross the oceans in dingy and over-crowded boats. Littoral nations such as Italy are a bursting of the seams with unwanted economics guests who have come in search of jobs that are not even die.

Many are tricked into slavery while others sell one in a family of many to raise capital for financing the fatalistic journey from which many have failed to return or reach their destinations.

People are in debt, slavery and seclusion as we speak, being either direct or indirect victims of the so-called economic migration.

TECHNICAL DIVORSES

Some marriages have become prison yards from which partners are wanting out but are trapped. The marriage has become a veil covering hate, domestic violence, cheating and hurtful insensitivity. People are living in bondage in such marriages and in some cases, in-law have intruded, turning the home into hell for their child-in-law.

Those who find themselves in those conditions and similar ones need to be rescued not from the marriage for marriage indeed is a good thing but people in and around the marriage. Counselors have a big role to play in homes particularly broken homes where people stay together just to keep up appearances.

INCREASING HUMAN TRAFFICKING-

Keeps landing hordes of persons deceived and blackmailed into landing on foreign shores and foster homes. These people are shell shocked when they discover that instead of honey pots, they have migrated from fry-pan to fire. Trafficked people are mostly on the same page as economic refugees.

Most times, these people cannot even come out in the open to seek help needed because of the fear of being arrested.

CHAPTER FOUR

WHY TELEPHONE COUNSELNG IN PARTICULAR?

It enables us to reach people who are too ashamed to come out in person. They call and talk on phone without eye contact.

People, especially women, who are held in "purdah" [Islamic seclusion] or other forms of religious captivity. They easily overcome this bias by calling.

It enables the high and mighty to call and not lose face, as they have been thinking in the case of in-person counseling

It reduces accusation of sexual trespasses. It may not eliminate such allegation completely but it certainly art ails t because there is no physical telephone in counseling.

It saves cost of traveling to the counseling center for the person being counseled.

If the phone is a free call, provided by charity, the caller is further served with a saving of his lean purpose.

It reaches people who are in prison or detention camps for whatever reason.

It enables us minister to persons who are in far and remote regions. Distance is no more a barrier especially with the global penetration of mobile telephony.

It reaches where we may not be allowed to enter in person. Some countries hinder missionaries and this can be circumvented when those in the mission fields have toll-free numbers they can call.

We can minister healing to the sick by sending the word of God over the phone. It is not the touching that heals in the case of religious healing but the sending of the word of God into the situation and circumstance.

It overcomes denominational bias which tends to make some not to go to ministries outside their own denomination.

It saves time of traveling for the caller.

It delivers people from telling lies by using the point above as excuse for not calling when not actually up to it.

Telephone counseling enables us to reach more people than in the physical or in person. A telephone counselor can have many persons who call him from time to time for counseling because of the reach.

Offerings can be made via mobile money or recharge cards. A woman I ministered to asked me whether she could send recharge cards to enable us reach more persons. I said why not? I do not know of anything in the Bible that stops you since it is a voluntary affair.

Record keeping is easier because some handsets keep record of callers and their details.

Some Apps can be attached to enable you to see each other e.g. **Skype.**

Anonymous experience and testimony sharing can be carried out via telephone group therapy e.g. **WhatsApp** groups.

Telephone counseling can always start small with just a handset already owned by a counselor. It does not require a large capital outlay to start.

Volunteers can pray from their homes. This ministry needs a lot of prayer backing and this can be provided by volunteers world-wide.

Telephone counseling can be kept open round the clock via telephone connectivity with volunteers world-wide.

It is a good evangelism tool because those healed might need a place to worship or be led to Christ on phone.

Donors to your ministry can always cross-check what you are doing by doing anonymous calls if needed.

Training of counselors can also be done cheaply on line. This will give people the chance to study without affecting their livelihood and other activities in the church.

It makes globalization of your ministry easier since telephone penetration is world-wide.

It is easier to have a referral system online or a telephone since new people do not need to make exploratory visits in person.

Most mobile line operators give bonus air-time and promos that can enable you reach more people with little or no extra charge.

When family therapy is involved, all lines in the family can be easily connected, if necessary.

A telephone counseling center uses mainly below-the-line advertising. In simple terms this means that the type of advertisement needed is not expensive and is as simple as cutting cardboards, writing on them with markers and pasting them where potential clients would see them or printing small call cards and distributing directly to potential callers.

Telephone counseling publicizes your ministry in more ways than in-person counseling. Mainly because of the global telephone penetration we have today. Mobile phones are now getting deeper and deeper into the remotest of villages in backward nations.

DISAVANTAGES

The points above should not in any way suggest that telephone counseling has no bones. Below are some known disadvantages.

Where line is not free, calls can be expensive; however can never be as expensive as the caller travelling to the center. Encourage those around the center to come in in-person.

Eye- contact is lost. Yes but one has to rely on the Holy Spirit in case of Christian counseling and what the client has to say.

Body language of the client is also lost. This can as well be handled by relying on what the client says or what Holy Spirit reveals as in point two above.

Crank callers who have no genuine purpose can call and keep calling to distract the counselor. Take note of them and block them. However, if the issue persists, I recommend prayers.

CHAPTER FIVE

ASSOCIATION AND MENTORING

A tree does not make a forest. Iron sharpens iron. Blessed is he that sits with the wise because he will learn. No man knows it all! My advice is look for a professional body, church, telephone or online counseling group to belong to for mentoring and probably certification. Such a group will help you in more ways than one.

I recommend IFCCC because I know them and there are things they can do for you. The very first counseling center established under IFCCC, is called "Lovelines" for short.

Permit to quote from one of their advertisement handbills,

"WHAT LOVE LINES WILL DO TO HELP

Love lines will share its experience and spiritual support by providing:

Director's Video training:

{we have 6 hours of training on how to operate a successful telephone counseling ministry}.

A printed Director's training manual of basic instructions with copies of all relevant forms.

Counselor training manual with 22 pertinent topics for counselor training.

Advice and counseling via the internet, e-mail, long distance telephone and fax as requested by the local counseling ministry.

A tie-in with other telephone counseling ministries throughout the world, through our global network fellowship.

<u>WHAT THE LOCAL MINISTRY NEEDS TO DO</u>

The local church or established Para-church ministry will pro-vide the local spiritual and organizational leadership.

 In addition, the local ministry will:

Select a paid, part time or full-time Director

Support the Director in recruiting qualified volunteers.

Raise the funds needed to pay for the Director, telephone lines, training materials and housing of a location where the telephone counseling will take place."

You can contact them on www.lovelines.org

NOTE: An existing telephone, at the local church or established Para-church ministry location, can be utilized at the start of the telephone counseling ministry. Further, a paid staff or person from the local church or established Para-church ministry can be selected as the director, provided, he/she has the calling of the Holy Spirit to be involved in the counseling ministry.

CHAPTER SIX

HOW TO START A TELEPHONE COUNSELING CENTER

Pray and be sure you are led by Holy Spirit to do this.

Set up prayer backing for this ministry. If a local church is available for this purpose that is far better than having a person praying alone.

Serve as the center director for a start.

Other persons can be employed later as the ministry develops.

Use your home or church as starting address. A telephone center can later grow into large buildings of its own as the work expands. Once you are called, do not allow the spirit of procrastination, excuse and perfection keep you from action.

Through you can start with your personal/normal telephone line, it is better to have a dedicated line for this purpose. That way, other business interests that you have may not be hampered by persistent calls that now go on the dedicated line. Remember that telephone ministry means making your line open to the public.

Print small cards e.g. call cards, telling people why they should call so-and –so number. For instance you can say:

 "Do you need healing? Call this Number: ---"

When properly distributed, those who need healing will get to know of the existence of the number and call.

Your advert message must be brief. We are in a busy world and there are millions of messages floating out there.

Message on the card you are sharing, must be to solve a problem. It is people who have problem that need your services.

  Word it carefully enough as to arouse interest! It should be boldly printed and direct to the point, telling the receiver what you do and what you want the person to do after reading the card.

Avoid putting the name of your local church to enable you over-come biases. Remember that some people from other denominations may not call once they know that you are of a different denomination. However, the taste of the pudding as they say is in the eating. When they call, and are pleased enough to want to call again, there will be time enough to give them your ministry address.

Message must be bold so everyone can lead it

Research and know where your prospects are and how best to meet them. While some can be reached by hitting the markets, others must be reached at the banks, to give just two examples.

 Share out your cards based on your research result. Do not distribute your cards without aim. Keep in view the type of clients you want to share. When you hand your card to the wrong persons, they litter the streets with them and in some cities; you may be fined for constituting public nuisance.

Make sure your phone lines are working. When people call once and do not get you or fail to hear you clearly due to channel noise, it will take desperation for them to try again. Re member that people discourage easily especially when they have other options. After all, you may not be the only counselor in town.

Keep an eye out for people you can recruit and train as volunteer counselors. That is a major way to ensure that the counseling center continues to expand to meet, if not outstrip, demand of your services.

Give lectures or talks in local churches on why a Christian should be available to counsel others, especially elders and mature Christians as volunteer!

Of course, volunteers can do so many other things like help clean the place or keep records. However, the best form of advertisement is the word of the mouth spoken in the right places.

Explore other forms of below the line advertising available in your area. Seek expert advice on this if need be.

Follow up on all who come for your services. If one person is satisfied, chances are that he or she will tell others.

Be focused and persistent. With time, the center will grow. Remember that the journey of a million miles starts with a small shot step.

If you are pasturing already, make sure that the
church is well aware of this center. They too will
tell their neighbors about it.

As time goes on, with the consent of the clients,
print fliers that include testimonies from your
counseling center. Do all you can to let people
know what God is doing in your center! The Bible
says that we overcome the devil with the
testimonies of our mouth.

OTHER BOOKS BY THE SAME AUTHOR.

Why A Christian Should Not Be Called Augustine.

How To Know A Mad Pastor.

14 Surprising Things We Do That Put

People Off Christianity.

4. . Why Many Pastors

5. Preach Beyond Allotted Time.

6. How To Pray Against Terrorism.

7. Hundred Things A Pastor

Can Do To Help Government

Rule Well.

8. 77 Benefits Of Foreign Missions.

9. How To Increase Your Ministerial

Connections.

10. Hundred Bad Thing Members Do To
Their Pastors.

THANK YOU

- for making out time to read this book. The author will appreciate your honest comments for the improvement of this book in subsequent editions.

For that purpose, kindly contact the author on:

Email: crediblewritersassociation@gmail.com

Thanks and God bless you.

NOTES

NOTES

www.ingramcontent.com/pod-product-compliance
Lightning Source LLC
Chambersburg PA
CBHW050707250726
48662CB00002B/886